A Book of Graces

D0679981

For David - I bought this little book from Whitfield for you, as I thought such a variety of graces might be useful for you. Mary

A Book of Graces

Compiled and edited by

DOROTHY M. STEWART

First published in Great Britain in 2009

Society for Promoting Christian Knowledge
36 Causton Street
London SW1P 4ST

Copyright © Dorothy M. Stewart 2009

All rights reserved. No part of this book may be reproduced or
transmitted in any form or by any means, electronic or
mechanical, including photocopying, recording, or by any
information storage and retrieval system, without permission
in writing from the publisher.

SPCK does not necessarily endorse the individual views
contained in its publications.

The author and publisher have made every effort to ensure that the
external website and email addresses included in this book are
correct and up to date at the time of going to press.
The author and publisher are not responsible for the content,
quality or continuing accessibility of the sites.

British Library Cataloguing-in-Publication Data
A catalogue record for this book is available from the British Library

ISBN 978–0–281–06095–5

1 3 5 7 9 10 8 6 4 2

Designed and typeset by Kenneth Burnley, Wirral, Cheshire
Printed in Great Britain by Ashford Colour Press

Produced on paper from sustainable forests

Contents

Introduction	*vi*
Short and sweet	1
The funny ones	8
Thank you for our food	12
Blessings plus	18
The Jewish tradition	27
National heritage	31
Latin graces	47
Derived from the Bible	50
Graces by the great and the good	53
Graces from times past	57
Remembering those who have less than we have	64
Formal and institutional graces	73
Special occasions: Weddings	79
Christmas	81
Thanksgiving	82
Harvest	85
Easter	88
Sung graces	89
Children's graces	93
Graces from other faiths and none	99
Grace after food	105
Acknowledgements	107
Index of authors	113
Index of first lines	115

Introduction

When SPCK asked me to compile this book of graces, I thought it would be a nice easy task. Surely graces abounded. As a child I'd been brought up with the remarkably graceless, 'For what we are about to receive may the Lord make us truly thankful.' I always thought it was a sad grace. If God had to make you thankful for the food, it obviously wasn't going to be very nice. And that was totally irrelevant in our house where my mother, who is an excellent cook, produced delicious meals seven days a week.

However, once I'd written down the few I knew, I set to with gusto, emailing everyone I could think of to request a grace – and was surprised at how few responded, or who actually emailed back to say they'd never said grace in their lives. (To those who did send graces, and then went on to network in others who also sent graces, I am very grateful and list them with my thanks in the Acknowledgements on page 107.)

Little daunted, I plunged into book research and was shocked to discover that, apart from books that were specifically collections of graces, we seem to be very spare with our gratitude for the food we eat. I found prayers for morning, prayers for bedtime, prayers for Christmas Day and presents – but few for the meals that surely the writers had consumed.

And this made me wonder: are we graceless people? Have we simply got out of the habit of saying thank you? Or do we think, since our food comes from the supermarket and we pay for it with our own hard-earned cash, there's no need to say thank you to God who seems even further down the supply chain than ever? Is this a symptom of the spiritual barrenness of consumerism?

I have therefore collected together in this book short graces for the sound-bite generation, funny graces for those with a funny bone, children's graces and foreign graces, graces from other faiths and none, graces that remember that there are still people starving today, and graces that simply celebrate the good things of life (I've called some of these Blessings plus). In this medley, I hope there will be something that will encourage regular grace-sayers and those who aren't in the habit of saying thank you to find a pleasing form of words to match their mood or their occasion.

I am reminded of the story about the atheist, which seems to pop up from time to time on the internet:

An atheist was wandering in some woods when a big grizzly bear appeared and got him in a tight hold.

'Oh God!' the atheist cried.

The wood went silent, time seemed to stop and the bear froze, claws at the man's throat. Suddenly there was a bright light and a voice from the sky. 'You've denied my existence all these years yet you expect me to help you now? Have you become a believer suddenly?'

The atheist replied, 'I'd be a hypocrite if I said I'd become a Christian, and asked you to save me, but could you make the bear a Christian?'

There was a silence. Then the voice came again. 'Very well. I shall do as you ask.'

The bright light faded away and the sounds of the wood resumed. The huge bear moved. He took his paws away from the man's throat, folded them together and said, 'Lord, bless this food, which I am about to receive from thy bounty; through Christ our Lord. Amen.'

Short and sweet

In a world where time is short and meals are often hurried, it can be hard even to remember to say grace, let alone find one that is suitable. The temptation is to say the same grace at every meal – which may get boring, or become a mere murmur of words, which does not produce that meaningful pause to consider the benefits of the food before us or the generosity of the Creator. Here is a very varied selection, from the extremely brief at only three words to a little longer, which may merit a place in your repertoire.

1   Thank you, Lord.
     Anonymous

2   Great, Pa.
     Ta.
     Traditional

3   Blessings on our meal.

Said by the whole family holding hands: often used in Steiner-inspired communities

4   Us
    and this,
    bless.
    Amen.

Traditional Quaker

5   Praise the Lord and pass the mustard.

Anonymous

6   Bless this food and us that eats it.

Cowboy grace

7   Good food,
    good meat,
    good God.
    Let's eat.

Anonymous

8   One word as good as ten –
     eat away.
     Amen.

     St Agnes, 291–304

9   Brown bread and the gospel is good fare.
     Amen.

     Matthew Henry, 1662–1714

10   For every cup and plateful,
     God make us truly grateful.

     Anonymous

11   May God be praised
     that all things be so good.
     Amen.

     John Donne, 1573–1631

12   For friends, family and the roast –
     praise Father, Son and Holy Ghost.

     Anonymous

13   Come, Lord Jesus, be our guest.
      Let this food to us be blest.

Traditional

14   Dear Lord,
      bless these sinners,
      as this day they eat their dinners.
      Amen.

Anonymous

15   You have given us so much, Lord.
      Help us to share it.
      Amen.

from Family Prayers, *1971*

16   For health and strength and daily food,
      we praise your name, O Lord.
      Amen.

Often used in Steiner-inspired communities

17   For what we are about to receive,
      may the Lord make us truly thankful.

Traditional

18   Bless me, O Lord,
       and let my food strengthen me
       to serve thee.
       Amen.
       Isaac Watts, 1674–1748

19   Give thanks to God with one accord
       for all that is set on this board.
       Amen.
       Primer, 1553

20   God bless our meat,
       God guide our ways,
       God give us grace
       our Lord to please.
       Amen.
       George Bellin, 1565

21   God sends no one away empty
       except those who are full of themselves.
       Thanks be to God.
       Amen.
       Dwight L. Moody, 1837–99

22   God's grace is the only grace
      and all grace is the grace of God.
      Thanks be to God.

Coventry Patmore, 1823–96

23   For these gifts of food,
      and for your care day by day,
      O Heavenly Father, we thank you.
      Amen.

F. W. Street

24   Lord, make us truly thankful
      for these and all other blessings.
      I ask this in Jesus Christ's name.
      Amen.

Traditional

25   Dear Lord, thank you for all you have given us.
      Please use and multiply what little we give to you.
      Amen.

from Family Prayers, *1971*

26   Dear Lord,
      we ask you to bless this food to our bodies
      and our lives to your service.
      In Jesus' name.
      Amen

      Traditional, Celeste Lotz

27   God is good,
      God is great!
      Let us thank him for our food.
      Bless the cook,
      bless the server,
      and bless the eater!
      In Jesus' name.
      Amen.

      Anonymous

The funny ones

I'm not sure I understand why we have funny graces though I am convinced that God has an excellent sense of humour. Following is a selection of the funniest, wittiest and most satirical graces I have found. Not surprisingly many of these come under the authorship of Anonymous. In many cases these graces have been passed on through the oral tradition and now in its modern-day form of the internet, the original author long forgotten.

28   For bread and jam
      and beans on toast,
      praise Father, Son
      and Holy Ghost.
      Amen.

      Anonymous

29 Dear Lord, please don't make us like porridge,
    which is difficult to stir and slow to serve.
    Make us instead like cornflakes,
    which are crisp and fresh and ready to serve.

    Boys' Brigade camp grace

30 In the name of the Father,
    Son and the Holy Ghost.
    Whoever eats the fastest
    gets the most!

    Anonymous

31 O Lord, heap blessings on the soup,
    Heap blessings on the stovies.*
    Heap blessings on the Papes and Jews,
    the Muslims and Jehovies.
    Heap blessings on all gathered here,
    on absent friends and strangers.
    And, if you've any blessings left,
    O God, please bless the Rangers.

    Allan Denholm, The West of Scotland Ecumenical Grace

*Stovies is a delicious way of using up the very last bits from a
roast of beef and involves beef dripping, onions and potatoes,
not to mention an enlarged waistline.

32   God!
If all you are is a swig, come into my throat!
If all you are is a loaf, come into my belly!

Gipsy prayer

33   When turkey's on the table laid,
and good things I may scan,
I'm thankful that I wasn't made
a vegetarian.

Edgar A. Guest, 1881–1959

34   The Lord be praised!
My belly is raised
one inch above the table,
and I'll be hanged
if I'm not crammed
as much as I am able.

Veronica Heley's grandfather, Nottingham, pre-1950s

35   Heavenly Father, bless us
and keep us all alive.
There's ten of us to dinner
and not enough for five.

Hodge's grace

36   God send this crumb well down.

Royalist grace during the Civil War period:
Cromwell was often pronounced Crumwell

37   Doon on your hunkers
and up wi' your paws.
Let's thank the Lord
for the use of your jaws.

A Scottish minister at a Scottish wedding

38   Gracious and glorious,
three slices 'tween four of us.
Thank God there's no more of us.
Amen.

Traditional

39   Praise to God who givest meat,
convenient unto all who eat.
Praise for tea and buttered toast.
Praise Father, Son and Holy Ghost.

Traditional

Thank you for our food

As I queue at the supermarket check-out, I'm always interested to see what's in other people's trolleys. Once upon a time, bread was our staple food – now it could be pasta, pizza, burgers. And ale was the old English drink when water was unsafe. Now, we are told, we have become accustomed to drinking wine. So here are graces focusing on our food, starting with our daily bread and moving on to include wine and more modern patterns of eating.

40   Blessed are you, great God,
        for you bring forth bread from the earth.
        Blessed are you, great God,
        for you have grown fruit from the vine.
        Blessed are you, great God,
        for you have brought us life.
        Amen.

Michael and Susan Durber

41   Our God,
     for all the good things you provide for us
     we are truly grateful.
     Help us to enjoy them now
     and remember that they come from you.
     Amen.

     Andrew Mayo

42   We thank you for our food;
     for the table laden for a celebration
     with the rich harvest of your earth;
     for the plates and dishes brimming over;
         we thank you for our food.

     We thank you for our food;
     for the bread and cheese by the roadside
     and the hurried snack on a journey;
     for the meal break in the working day;
         we thank you for our food.

     We thank you for our food;
     the colour and texture of ingredients,
     the tang of herbs and the smell of spices,
     the satisfaction of preparing a tasty meal;
         we thank you for our food.

We thank you for our hunger;
for the anticipation of a meal to end the day,
for the work, which increases our appetite,
and our sense of taste and savour;
   we thank you for our hunger.

Lord Jesus Christ, you knew hunger and thirst
and you fed the souls and bodies of those who
   came to you in Galilee;
give us food and friends to share it at our table
   day by day;
share with us your concern for the unfed;
and unite all in your company who break bread
   at your table.
Amen.

Stephen Orchard

43   Lord,
   may we share this meal with the same
   joy, thankfulness, humour and awareness
   that Jesus showed
   when he ate and drank with his friends.
   May our eating and drinking be a sign of life
   in your kingdom of forgiveness and peace.
   Amen.

David Jenkins

44 We pray that as we share this meal
we'll learn the new command you give
that by the way we grow in love
we'll show that we belong to you.
Amen.

Chris Warner

45 Bountiful God, bless this food
and feed us in our eating.
Make this meal a sacrament of meeting.

Jean Mortimor

46 Forgive us our hurried, inhospitable lifestyle
of fast food and take-away snacks,
which takes the edge off appetite
without satisfying our need for conversation and
companionship.
Forgive our reliance on instant, convenient,
flavourless eating,
which keeps life bland and easy to digest.
Give us the stomach to sit at your table
to eat, drink and share till all are replete.

Jean Mortimor

47 Many grains, many grapes,
   bread broken and wine poured,
   food of earth and heaven,
   gathering and uniting us
   as Christ's body in God's world.
   We give you thanks . . .
   Amen.

   Claire McBeath

48 Thank you for the miracle of a good wine;
   the grapes on sunny slopes,
   the juice fermenting in the vat,
   the nose and the flavours,
   the colours and the tipsiness.
   Thank you for the table wine, the fine wine,
   the bubbly and the solemn wine.
   Thank you for the freedom and the friendliness,
   the passion and the pleasure,
   of good and wonderful wine.
   Glory to God when water turns to wine!
   Amen.

   Michael and Susan Durber

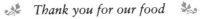

49   As food is shared among us,
      in our homes, in cafés or restaurants,
      in a picnic in the park or a business lunch,
      in a fellowship supper or in Holy Communion,
      let us pray that its calories and its context
      will give us strength
      to live for one another and for God,
      so that, one day, all God's children may be fed
      and taste at last the food of eternal life.
      Amen.

Michael and Susan Durber

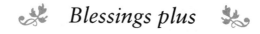 *Blessings plus*

While saying grace may have begun as a way to give thanks to God for food about to be received, graces have developed and expanded into prayers of thanksgiving for the many more blessings we receive. Which is why I've called this section 'Blessings plus'.

50 Jesus, thank you for loving us
    and providing food, shelter, and one another.
    Every moment of our lives is a gift
    and we appreciate all the time you have given us.
    Thank you for all our good fortune.
    Amen.
    Anonymous

51 For these and his other mercies,
    above all, the crowning mercy of serious
         conversation,
    God's name be praised.
    Alfred Austin, 1835–1913

52 My eyes praise the Lord!
    Look how wonderful God is.
    My stomach praises the Lord!
    Look how generous God is.
    My hands praise the Lord!
    Look how gentle God is.
    My mouth praises the Lord!
    I will worship God for ever.

    Chris Campbell

53 As we look forward to the glory of your kingdom
    we give thanks for the love that surrounds us
    and the healing comfort you bring.
    Amen.

    Melanie Frew

54 For life and love, for rest and food,
    for daily help and nightly care,
    sing to the Lord, for he is good,
    and praise his name, for it is fair.

    John Samuel Bewley Monsell, 1811–75

55   Whatever we do, you are with us;
whether we eat or drink, write or work,
read, meditate, or pray, you are ever with us;
wherever we are or whatever we do,
we feel some measure of your mercies and love.
If we are oppressed, you defend us.
If we hunger, you feed us.
Whatever we need, you give us.
Oh continue your loving-kindness towards us
    for ever,
that all the world may see your power, your
    mercy and your love,
in which you have never failed us,
that all shall see that your mercies endure
    for ever;
through Jesus Christ your Son our Lord.
Amen.

J. Norden

56   God, you nourish and sustain us
all through our lives.
Each breath of air, each drop of water
and each crumb of bread comes from your hand.
Your Spirit takes the dust and breathes it into life.

You feed our imagination, so that eyes and ears
    and hands
respond to new sensations every second.
When all our being takes your gifts of every kind
and in our daily life we find one glad wholeness,
a sense that all is right and good because you
    bless it,
we are most truly fed.

Stephen Orchard

57   My God, I thank thee, who hast made
the earth so bright,
so full of splendour and of joy,
beauty and light!
So many glorious things are here,
noble and right!

I thank thee, too, that thou hast made
joy to abound,
so many gentle thoughts and deeds
circling us round
that in the darkest spot on earth
some love is found.

Adelaide Anne Procter, 1825–64

58   Lord God, people need food –
      we remember before you all those near and
          far away
      who have worked hard to ensure that we have
          enough to eat today.
      People enjoy food –
      we remember with gratitude those very special
          meals,
      with trusted friends, on festive occasions,
          at times of celebration.
      People need more than food –
      we remember before you all those who have
          made the Bible enticing for us,
      through the fragrance of their lives and
          through the attraction of their words.
      People enjoy more than food –
      we remember with gratitude those very special
          times when,
      in casual moments or intentional listening,
          we have sensed your words with us.
      Please continue to sustain us with your truths
      and help us to share your story with others
      so that they, too, can be nourished for their
          journey.

We ask this through Jesus Christ our Lord.
Amen.

David Spriggs

59 Lord, I would own thy tender care,
and all thy love to me;
the food I eat, the clothes I wear,
are all bestowed by thee.

Jane Taylor, 1783–1824

60 For food that stays our hunger,
for rest that brings us ease,
for homes where memories linger,
we give our thanks for these.

Traditional

61 May thy Holy Spirit continually descend
and rest upon all in this house
and upon all who are in any way connected with it.
Send down thy blessing upon our food,
and keep us this day in body and soul;
for the sake of Jesus Christ our Lord.
Amen.

H. W. Turner

62   Lord Jesus Christ,
          who came to earth that we might have life,
          and that we might have it more abundantly,
          give us the capacity always to enjoy your gifts
                to us,
          and especially the gift of life itself,
          that through these gifts we may learn
          to enjoy the supreme gift of eternal life,
          shared for ever with you and the Father and the
                Holy Spirit,
          world without end.
          Amen.
          Andrew Warner

63   For all the glory of the way,
          for your protection, night and day,
          for roof-tree, fire and bed and board,
          for friends and home,
          we thank you, Lord.
          Amen.
          Wayfarer's grace

64   Give me a good digestion, Lord,
          and also something to digest.

Give me a healthy body, Lord,
and sense to keep it at its best.
Give me a healthy mind, good Lord,
to keep the good and pure in sight;
which, seeing sin, is not appalled,
but finds a way to set it right.
Give me a mind that is not bound,
that does not whimper, whine or sigh.
Don't let me worry overmuch
about the fussy thing called 'I'.
Give me a sense of humor, Lord;
give me the grace to see a joke,
to get some happiness from life
and pass it on to other folk.

Thomas H. B. Webb

65   O Lord of heaven and earth and sea,
to thee all praise and glory be;
how shall we show our love to thee,
who givest all?

For peaceful homes and healthful days,
for all the blessings earth displays,
we owe thee thankfulness and praise,
who givest all.

Christopher Wordsworth, 1807–85

66   Living Love,
      beginning and end,
      giver of food and drink,
      clothing and warmth,
      love and hope:
      life in all its goodness –
      we praise and adore you.
      Brian Wren

67   I am blessed,
      I am blessed.
      Every day of my life
      I am blessed.
      When I wake up in the morning,
      when I lay my head to rest,
      I am blessed,
      I am blessed.
      Traditional breakfast grace

The Jewish tradition

Our older brothers and sisters in the faith have much to teach us about saying thank you to God. After all, it is they whom he originally taught about himself, their story that informs our thinking about God and was the fertile spiritual heritage of Jesus. Following are age-old and modern thanksgivings from the Jewish tradition.

68   Blessed are you, O Lord our God, eternal King,
      who feeds the whole world with your goodness,
      with grace, with loving-kindness and with
            tender mercy.
      You give food to all flesh,
      for your loving-kindness endures for ever.
      Through your great goodness, food has never
            failed us.
      Oh may it not fail us for ever, for your name's
            sake,

since you nourish and sustain all living things,
and do good to all,
and provide food for all your creatures
whom you have created.
Blessed are you, O Lord, who gives food to all.

A Hebrew blessing

69 Blessed art thou, O Lord our God,
    King of the universe,
who createst the fruit of the vine.
Blessed art thou, O Lord our God,
    King of the universe,
who createst various kinds of food.
Blessed art thou, O Lord our God,
    King of the universe,
who createst the fruit of the earth.
Blessed art thou, O Lord our God,
    King of the universe,
by whose word all things exist.
Amen.

From the Hebrew Prayer Book

70 Blessed be the Lord God of the universe,
    by whose goodness we live
    and by whose bounty we eat.
    Amen.

    Traditional

71 Blessed be thou, Lord God of the universe,
    who bringest forth bread from the earth,
    and makest glad the hearts of your people.
    Amen.

    Traditional

72 For the food we are about to eat,
    and for all that sustains us,
    we give thanks to the creator and sustainer of life.
    Amen.

    Contemporary

73   Though our mouths were full of song as the sea,
      and our tongues of exultation as the multitude
            of its waves,
      and our lips of praise as the wide-extended
            firmament;
      though our eyes shone with light like the sun
            and the moon,
      and our hands were spread forth like the
            eagles of heaven,
      and our feet were swift as hinds,
      we should still be unable to thank you and
            bless your name,
      O Lord our God and God of our fathers and
            mothers,
      for one thousandth or one ten-thousandth part
            of the bounties
      that you have bestowed upon our forebears
            and upon us.
      Amen.

      Traditional

National heritage

One of the joys of travel is discovering and tasting the cuisines of other countries, delightful evidence of the variety embedded in God's creation. Maybe the different foods we eat and the new cultures we experience are part of the filter through which we experience God. Just as we can step outside our own cultures and enjoy different food, so we can step outside and share in a different approach to saying thank you.

Scots

74 Some hae meat and canna eat,
    and some wad eat that want it,
    but we hae meat and we can eat,
    so let the Lord be thankit.
Robert Burns, The Selkirk Grace

75   O thou who kindly dost provide
      for every creature's want,
      we bless thee, God of nature wide,
      for all thy goodness lent.
      And if it please thee, heavenly Guide,
      may never worse be sent;
      but, whether granted or denied,
      Lord, bless us with content.
      Robert Burns, 1759–96

76   Every thing I have received, from thee it came.
      Each thing for which I hope, from thy love
          it will come.
      Each thing I enjoy, it is of thy bounty.
      Each thing I ask, comes of thy disposing.
      Amen.
      Gaelic prayer

77   Bless to me, O God,
      each thing my eye sees.
      Bless to me, O God,
      each sound my ear hears.

Bless to me, O God,
each odour that goes to my nostrils.
Bless to me, O God,
each taste that goes to my lips.
Amen.

Prayer from the Western Isles

78 The Sacred Three
    my fortress be,
    encircling me.
    Come and be round
    my hearth,
    my home.
    Amen.

Hebridean chant

79 Without your sunshine and your rain,
    we would not have your golden grain.
    Without your love, we'd not be fed:
    we thank you for our daily bread.
    Amen.

Traditional Gaelic

80   Our God, we are your guests,
and 'tis you who keeps this generous table.
We thank you.
Amen.

Isle of Lewis blessing

81   Bless the sheep for David's sake;
he herded sheep himself.
Bless the fish for Peter's sake;
he netted fish himself.
Bless the swine for Satan's sake;
he was once a swine himself.
Amen.

Old Galloway grace

Celtic (Scottish or Irish)

82   Thank you, God,
for blue skies above,
green grass below,

good friends beside,
fine food in front,
and peace,
wherever it is found.
Amen.

83   May the blessing
of the five loaves and the two fish
be ours also.
May we be counted among the five thousand
who ate and drank to their fill
and yet found enough to share beyond.
Amen.

84   The Sacred Three be blessing thee,
this table and its store.
The Sacred Three be blessing
all your loved ones evermore.
Amen.

Yorkshire

85   O Lord, make us able
      to eat all food
      that's put ont table.
      Traditional

Irish

86   I ask for the angels of heaven to be among us.
      I ask for the abundance of peace.
      I ask for full vessels of charity.
      I ask for rich treasures of mercy.
      I ask for cheerfulness to preside over all.
      I ask for Jesus to be present.
      Brigid (Bride), d. c. 523

87   We ask thy blessing, gracious God,
              as we sit together.
      We ask thy blessing on the food we eat this day.
      We ask thy blessing on the faithful hands that
              made the food
      and on ourselves.
      This we pray.
      Amen.

Europe

88   O God, who makes a thousand flowers to blow,
who makes both grains and fruits to grow,
hear our prayer:
    bless this food
    and bring us peace.
Amen.

Dutch

89   *Père eternel, qui nous ordonnes n'avoir souci du*
    lendemain, des biens que pour ce jour nous
    donnes te mercions de coeur humain.
    Or, puisqu'il t'a plu, de ta main, donner au
    corps manger et boire, plaise-toi du céleste
    pain paître nos âmes, à ta gloire. Amen.

Eternal Father, who commands us not to worry
    about tomorrow, we give you thanks from
    human hearts for the things you've given us
    today. Now, since it has pleased you, with
    your hand to give food and drink for the
    body, may it please you to feed our souls with
    the heavenly bread, to your glory. Amen.

French, Clément Marot, 1496–1544

90   *Alle guten Gaben, alles was wir haben, kommt,*
     oh Gott, von dir. Dank sei dir dafür.

     All good gifts, all we have, comes from you,
         O Lord. We thank you for it.
     German, trans. Kirsten Weissenberg

91   *Komm, Herr Jesus, sei du unser Gast und segne,*
     was du uns bescheret hast.

     Come, dear Jesus, be our guest and bless what
         you have provided for us.
     German, trans. Kirsten Weissenberg

92   Lord Jesus,
     be with us in this,
     as in all things,
     for your name's sake.
     Amen.
     German, Martin Luther, 1485–1546

93   Bless us, O God the Father, who hast created us.
Bless us, O God the Son, who hast redeemed us.
Bless us, O God the Holy Spirit, who sanctifieth us.
O Blessed Trinity, keep us in body, soul and spirit
        unto everlasting life.
Amen.

Weimarisches Gesangbuch, 1873

94   Thank Heaven for this food
and for this company.
May it be good for us.
Amen.

Greek

95   O God,
how lovely it is to be your guest,
to taste of your fruit
and be blessed by your hand.
For the promise of dawn's awakening,
and the peace of evening rest –
and in between, the sustenance of food and
        friends – we give you praise.
Glory to you for the feast that is life.
Amen.

Russian, Gregory Petrov, d. c. 1942

96 As to the different kinds of food,
    we should take a little of everything, even sweets . . .
    We should never pick and choose,
    or push food aside,
    but should thank God for everything.
    Russian, Nilus Sorsky, c. 1433–1508

97 With bread and wine,
    we can walk the road.
    Thanks be to God.
    Spanish proverb

Asia

98 Each time we eat,
    may we remember God's love.
    Amen.
    Chinese

Africa

99 All you big things, bless the Lord –
    Mount Kilimanjaro and Lake Victoria,
    the Rift Valley and the Serengeti Plain,

fat baobabs and shady mango trees,
all eucalyptus and tamarind trees,
bless the Lord,
praise and extol God for ever and ever.
All you tiny things, bless the Lord –
busy black ants and hopping fleas,
wriggling tadpoles and mosquito larvae,
flying locusts and tsetse flies,
pollen dust and water drops,
millet seeds and dried dagaa,
bless the Lord,
praise and extol God for ever and ever.

from African Canticle

100 You have created all creatures with your word.
You carry them all without being weary,
and feed them all without ceasing.
You think of them all without forgetting any.
You watch over all without sleeping.
You hear us all without neglecting any.
Praise be to you.
Amen.

Ethiopian Orthodox, alt.

101 *Awadifo, Yesu,*
awadifo, Yesu,
awadifo, Yesu, nyakasi.
Thank you, Jesus,
thank you, Jesus,
thank you for our food.

Lugbara (Uganda), Keith and Margaret Rowbory

New Zealand

102 The food we have here is a gift
of air and earth and sea.
As we eat it, we take
on their life and energy.
Thank you, air.
Thank you, earth.
Thank you, sea.
Thank you, thou,
who gives all three.

Joy Cowley

103 Life is for living.
    Love is for giving.
    Friends are for caring.
    Food is for sharing.
    For food, friends, life and love,
    and for your life in us,
    O God, we thank you.
    Amen.

Joy Cowley

104 O thou, great giver of all things,
    give us grateful hearts.

Joy Cowley

United States of America

105 O Lord, now bless and bind us,
    and put old Satan 'hind us.
    Oh, let your Spirit mind us.
    Don't let none hungry find us.

African-American folk rhyme, 18th century

106 May all we say and all we think
be in harmony with you,
God within, God beyond me,
maker of all good things.
Amen.

Chinook Psalter

107 Lord,
we work mighty hard for these here vittals,
but we thank thee, just the same.
Amen.

Early pioneer grace, 1840s

108 For each new morning with its light,
for rest and shelter of the night,
for health and food,
for love and friends,
for everything thy goodness sends.

Ralph Waldo Emerson, 1803–82

109 Great God, accept our gratitude,
for the great gifts on us bestowed –
for raiment, shelter and for food.
Great God, our gratitude we bring,

accept our humble offering.
For all thy gifts on us bestowed,
thy name be evermore adored.

Josephine Delphine Henderson Heard, 1861–1921

110 Thank you for the wind and rain
and the sun and pleasant weather;
and thank you now for this our food
and that we are together.
Amen.

Mennonite

111 Come, Lord Jesus, our guest to be
and bless these gifts bestowed by thee.
Bless our loved ones everywhere
and keep them in your loving care.
Amen.

Moravian

112 Bless this food we are about to receive.
Give bread to those who hunger,
and hunger for justice to us who have bread.
Amen.

Traditional

113 For all your goodness, God,
   we give you thanks:
   thanks for the food we eat,
   and for the friends we meet;
   for each new day we greet,
   we give you thanks.
   Amen.

   Traditional

114 God is great,
   God is good,
   and we thank him for our food.
   By his hand we are fed.
   Give us, Lord, our daily bread.

   Traditional, probably learned by most people in the USA during childhood

Latin graces

Praying in our own language came late in western Christendom. From early on, since Latin was the language of the Roman Empire, it became the language of the established Church as well as the State (here is not the place to review the pervasive cultural colonialism of missionary Christianity!). Later, when the Empire had long vanished, Latin remained in use for formal and ceremonial occasions. Many Latin graces continue in use to this day and the same graces are considered 'the' grace of several schools and organizations. According to Professor Sir John Baker of St Catharine's College, Cambridge, many of these derive from the *Sarum Manual* and are variants of the same prayer.

115   *Benedic nobis, Dominum, et omnibus donis tuis,*
          quae ex larga liberalitate tua sumpturi sumus,
          per Dominum nostrum Jesum Christum.
      Amen.

      Forest Fields Grammar School, Nottingham, and St
      Catharine's College, Cambridge

116 *Benedicat nobis, omnipotens Deus, et doni qui*
per Dei laecetate praesumus percepturi,
per Jesum Christum, Dominum nostrum.
Amen.

St Peter's College, Oxford

117 *Benedictus benedicat.*
May the Blessed One give a blessing.

St Edward's School, Oxford; Westminster School, London;
Queens' College, Cambridge; British Legal Society

118 *Benedicatur.*
Amen.

The formula response

119 *Dominus Jesus,*
sit potus et esus.
Amen.

Lord Jesus,
be drink and food.
Amen.

Martin Luther, 1485–1546

120 *Oculi omnium in te sperant Domine:*
tu das iis escam eorum in tempore opportuno.
Aperis tu manum tuam:
et imples omne animal benedictione tua.
Sanctifica nos, quaesumus, Domine, per verbum
et orationem, istisque tuis donis, quae de tua
bonitate sumus accepturi, benedicito
per Christum Dominum nostrum.
Amen.

The eyes of all await upon thee, O Lord,
and thou givest them their food in due season.
Thou openest thy hand,
and fillest every living thing with thy blessing.
Sanctify us, we beseech thee, O Lord,
by thy word and our petition;
and bless the gifts which of thy bounty we
are about to receive; through Christ our Lord.
Amen.

Said in formal hall, Clare College, Cambridge

Derived from the Bible

Not only has the Bible much to teach us about gratitude, it also offers prayers and inspiration for prayers of thanksgiving. You might like to consider the following prayers and graces as encouragements for getting back to the Bible and creating your own.

121 Now therefore, our God, we thank thee
     and praise thy glorious name.

     1 Chronicles 29.13 (AV)

122 Even though we walk through the darkest valley,
     we fear no evil,
     for God is with us.
     God prepares a table before us;
     the oil of gladness is poured out,
     our cup overflows,
     goodness and mercy follow us always.
     Thanks be to God.
     Amen.

     23rd Psalm grace

123 Blessed be the Lord,
who daily loadeth us with benefits,
even the God of our salvation.

Psalm 68.19 (AV)

124 Thank you, Lord, for your promise of old,
'Open your mouth wide and I will fill it.'
Thank you for fulfilling it now.

Simon Baynes, from Psalm 81.10

125 Bless, O my soul, the Lord thy God,
and not forgetful be
of all his gracious benefits
he hath bestowed on thee.
who with abundance of good things
doth satisfy thy mouth;
so that, even as the eagle's age,
renewed is thy youth.

from Psalm 103.2, 5

126 Lord, make us mindful of those in need; according
to your promise, fill the hungry with good
things.

Simon Baynes, from Psalm 107.9

127 O Lord, thou art my God and King;
    thee will I magnify and praise:
    I will thee bless, and gladly sing,
    unto thy holy name always.

    from Psalm 145.1–2

128 The eyes of all wait upon thee;
    and thou givest them their meat in due season.
    Thou openest thine hand,
    and satisfiest the desire of every living thing.

    from Psalm 145.15, 16, known as the Fearon grace. This is the passage on which many College graces are based.

129 Thank you, Lord, for our daily bread; forgive us
    our debt to the needy of the world.

    Simon Baynes, from Matthew 6.11–12

130 Thank you, Lord, for rain and fruitful seasons;
    as you have given us food, so give us joy.

    Simon Baynes, from Acts 14.17

Graces by the great and the good

In this section you'll find some famous names, not only of the Christian faith but of literature and history. It's interesting to see how many of the 'great and good' bothered to say thank you to God for their food and all their blessings. I wonder how many of today's superstars would be able to contribute a personal grace if asked!

131 God bless our going out,
    nor less our coming in,
    and make them sure.
    God bless our daily bread,
    and bless whate'er we do
    whate'er endure.
    In death until his peace awake us,
    and heirs of his salvation make us.
    attr. Prince Albert, Prince Consort, 1819–61

132 O thou light of my heart,
   thou bread of my inmost soul,
   thanks be to thee,
   my joy and my glory,
   my confidence and my God,
   thanks be to thee for all thy gifts.

   St Augustine, 354–430

133 There is no such thing as 'my' bread.
   All bread is ours and is given to me,
   to others through me and to me through others.
   Thanks be to God.

   Meister Eckhart, c. 1260–1327

134 Lord Jesus, be our holy guest,
   our morning prayer,
   our evening rest,
   and with this daily food impart
   thy love and grace
   to every heart.
   Amen.

   President Dwight D. Eisenhower's grace

135 May he that feeds all things with his bounty
   command his blessing

upon what is or shall be
set upon this table.
Desiderius Erasmus, 1467–1536

136 Give us grace, O God,
to be ever thankful for your providence,
with hearts always ready to provide
for the needs of others.
St Francis of Assisi, 1182–1226

137 These things, good Lord, that we pray for,
give us thy grace to labour for.
Amen.
Thomas More, 1478–1535

138 O Lord, that lends me life,
lend me a heart replete with thankfulness.
William Shakespeare, 1564–1616

139 Lord, behold our family here assembled.
We thank thee for this place in which we dwell,
for the love that unites us,
for the peace accorded us this day,
for the health, the work, the food,

and the bright skies that make our lives delightful,
for our friends in all parts of the earth.
Give us courage, gaiety and the quiet mind.

Spare to us our friends,
soften to us our enemies.
Bless us, if it may be, in all our innocent endeavours.
If it may not, give us the strength
to encounter that which is to come.
May we be brave in peril,
constant in tribulation, temperate in wrath,
and in all changes of fortune
loyal and loving to one another.

Robert Louis Stevenson, 1850–94

140 Blessing to God, for ever blest,
to God the Master of the feast,
who hath for us a table spread,
and with his daily bounties fed;
may he with all his gifts impart
the crown of all – a thankful heart.
Amen.

Charles Wesley, 1707–88

Graces from times past

In my researches, I've been surprised and delighted by the way our predecessors in the faith seemed to be more ready than our generation to give God thanks. I was also surprised by how modern their sentiments were. Maybe we can learn a thing or two from the old books of prayers and the long-ago praying people.

141 It is meet before we partake of food
     to bless the maker of all things,
     and to sing when drinking.
     Clement of Alexandria, c. 150–c. 215

142 You are the guest who filled the jars with
         good wine,
     fill my mouth with your praise.
     Ephraem the Syrian, c. 306–73

143 Blessed God,
    who feedest me from my youth up,
    who givest food to all flesh,
    fill our hearts with joy and gladness,
    that always having all sufficiency,
    we may abound unto every good work in
      Jesus Christ our Lord,
    with whom be unto thee glory, honour and might,
    with the Holy Spirit for ever.
    Amen.

St John Chrysostom, 347–407

144 Satisfied, O Lord, with the gifts of thy riches,
    we give thee thanks for these things
    which we receive from thy bounty;
    beseeching thy mercy that
    that which was needful for our bodies
    may not be burdensome to our minds;
    through Jesus Christ our Lord.
    Amen.

Gelasian Sacramentary, 7th/8th century

145 Good Lord, for thy grace meekly we call,
   bless us and our meals and drinks withal.
   Amen.

Salisbury Primer, 1536

— Said before the St John's
Singers' Christmas Dinner
at the Red Lion: 10 Jan 2011

146 For these and all thy mercies given,
   we bless and praise thy name, O Lord!
   May we receive them with thanksgiving,
   ever trusting in thy word.
   To thee alone be honour, glory,
   now and henceforth, evermore.
   Amen.

from the Laudi Spirituali, *1545*

147 Pray we to God, the almighty Lord,
   that sendeth food to beasts and men,
   to send his blessings on this board,
   to feed us now and ever.
   Amen.

Primer, 1553

148 The eyes of all things do look up and trust in
       thee, O Lord.

Thou givest them their meat in due season,
thou dost open thy hand and fillest with thy
     blessings everything living.
Good Lord, bless us and all thy gifts,
which we receive of thy bounteous liberality;
through Jesus Christ our Lord.
Amen.

Queen Elizabeth's Primer, 1558

149 Almighty God, eternal King,
which madest heaven and every thing:
grant unto us that present be
to taste the food that here we see.

George Bellin, 1565

150 Bless these thy gifts, most gracious God,
from whom all goodness springs;
make clean our hearts and feed our souls
with good and joyful things.

Elizabethan Primer, 1580

151 Here a little child I stand
heaving up my either hand.

Cold as paddocks* though they be
still I lift them up to thee,
for a benison to fall
on our meat and on us all.
Robert Herrick, 1591–1674
*Paddocks: toads

152 What God gives, and what we take,
'Tis a gift for Christ his sake:
be the meal of beans and pease,
God be thanked for those and these;
have we flesh or have we fish
all are fragments from his dish.
He his Church save, and the King,
and our peace here, like a spring,
make it ever flourishing.
Robert Herrick, 1591–1674

153 Blessings we enjoy daily, and for the most of them,
because they be so common, men forget to pay
their praises.
But let not us,
because it is a sacrifice so pleasing to him who
still protects us,

61

and gives us flowers, and showers, and meat
    and content.
Amen.

Izaak Walton, 1593–1683

154 Great God, thou giver of all good,
accept our praise and bless our food;
grace, health and strength to us afford;
through Jesus Christ, our risen Lord.
Amen.

Jeremiah Clarke, 1674–1707

155 Thou who hast given so much to me,
give one thing more,
a grateful heart,
for Christ's sake.
Amen.

George Herbert, 1593–1633

156 All praise and glory is due to thee, O God,
which dost load us continually with thy mercies,
and has at this time plentifully fed our vile bodies:
we beseech thee to feed our souls with thy
    precious word,
which is the bread of life,

and make us truly thankful for all thy mercies;
for the sake of Jesus Christ our Lord.
Amen.

from Nathaniel Strong's England's Perfect Schoolmaster,
1699

157 O God, who givest food unto all flesh,
    grant that we may receive these thy gifts with thy
        blessing,
    and use them with sobriety and thankfulness;
    through Jesus Christ our Lord.
    Amen.

Thomas Wilson, Bishop of Sodor and Man, 1697–1755

158 May the grace of Christ our Saviour,
    and the Father's boundless love,
    with the Holy Spirit's favour,
    rest upon us from above.

John Newton, 1725–1807

159 Be present at our table, Lord,
    be here and everywhere ador'd:
    thy creatures bless and grant that we
    may feast in Paradise with thee.

John Cennick, 1718–55

Remembering those who have less than we have

In our rich western world, it can be hard really to imagine or understand what true poverty is like – despite the pictures in our newspapers and on our TV screens. Somehow the media sanitizes and distances poverty and injustice. Yet we are called to demonstrate God's bias towards the poor and disadvantaged. Mealtimes, when we rejoice in our plenty, can be an especially salutary time to remember our responsibility to those who have less than us.

160   Father, we thank thee for this food,
         for health and strength and all things good.
         May others all these blessings share,
         and hearts be grateful everywhere.
         Amen.
         Anonymous, 18th century

161 God, you heap your love upon us
   like a mother providing for her family's need,
   embracing her child with tenderness.

   Forgive us
   when, like spoilt children,
   we treat your generosity as our right,
   or hug it possessively to ourselves.

   Give us enough trust to live secure in your love
   and to share it freely with others
   in open-handed confidence
   that your grace will never run out.

   Jan Berry

162 Creator God,
   you have provided man with everything he needs
          for life and health.
   Grant that the resources of the earth may not be
          hoarded by the selfish
   or squandered by the foolish,
   but that all may share your gifts;
   through our Lord Jesus Christ.
   Amen.

   M. H. Botting's collection

163 In a world where there is so much hunger,
   we give thanks for food;
   in a world in which there is so much loneliness,
   we give thanks for friends;
   and in a world in which there is so much to do,
   we ask for strength to spend ourselves in
       Christ's service.
   Amen.

   Boys' Brigade

164   Generous God,
               thank you for feeding us.

For big stores and   *for busy market days and*
supermarkets and corner   *scattered roadside stalls*
shops open all hours

               generous God,
           thank you for feeding us.

For farms on land and   *for good landlords,*
loch and market   *family plots and*
gardens   *village co-ops*

               generous God,
           thank you for feeding us.

For high-yield seeds,   *for irrigation, tractors*
fertilizers and pesticides   *and new cash crops*

        generous God,
    thank you for feeding us.

For our standard of   *for survival in spite of*
living with food to   *erosion, loss of fertility*
spare for pets   *and poor crops*

        generous God,
    thank you for feeding us.

For surplus wealth sent   *for the charity of the*
as aid to feed the hungry   *west – so little for so*
of the world   *many*

        generous God,
    thank you for feeding us.

For the world's produce   *for breath to pray*
filling cupboards and   *despite poverty,*
freezers   *disease and hunger*

        generous God,
    thank you for feeding us.
            Amen.

Tony Burnham

165 God of the earth,
God of humanity,
we join hands to bless this food;
we join hands to bless one another.

We thank you for the hands that have prepared
this meal:
shopping, washing, cutting, chopping, stirring,
arranging, baking . . .
in this home and outside this home.
Bless these hands; we are one circle.
We thank you for the hands that have grown and
brought this food:
tilling, planting, picking, milking, processing,
counting, wrapping, carrying . . .
in nearby fields and factories and in fields and
factories far away.
Bless these hands; we are one circle.
We thank you for the hands of our circle
that join together in thanksgiving.
We cry out to you for the empty hands that plead
for mercy,
for food, for rest, for employment.
Bless these hands; we are one circle.
God of the earth,

God of all humanity,
teach us that we are one circle.
Bless this food that we may see it
as a sign of our interdependence
and as a call to use these hands of ours,
blessed by this community and this food,
so that all may have bread.
Amen.

Christina J. DelPiero

166 God our creator,
you have made us one with this earth,
to tend it and to bring forth fruit;
may we so respect and cherish
all that has life from you,
that we may share in the labour of all creation
to give birth to your hidden glory;
through Jesus Christ.
Amen.

Janet Morley

167 O God, when I have food,
   help me to remember the hungry;
when I have work,
   help me to remember the jobless;

when I have a home,
  help me to remember those who have no home
    at all;
when I am without pain,
  help me to remember those who suffer,
  and remembering,
  help me to destroy my complacency,
  bestir my compassion,
  and be concerned enough to help,
  by word and deed,
  those who cry out for what we take for granted.
Amen.

Samuel F. Pugh

168 Lord Jesus Christ,
because you broke bread with the poor,
you were looked on with contempt.

Because you broke bread with the sinful and the
    outcast,
you were looked on as ungodly.

Because you broke bread with the joyful,
you were called a winebibber and a glutton.

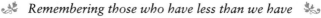

Because you broke bread in the upstairs room,
you sealed your acceptance of the way of the cross.

Because you broke bread on the road to Emmaus,
you made scales fall from the disciples' eyes.

Because you broke bread and shared it,
we will do so too,
and ask your blessing.

*from daily worship of 'Your Will be Done – Mission in
Christ's Way', San Antonio conference, 1990*

169 May God give us grateful hearts
and keep us mindful
of the needs of others.
Tasha Tudor

170 Provider God,
you are the source of all that is good.
From you comes food for body and spirit.

Forgive us that we forget this so easily.
Forgive us that, having stored up your resources,
we then think that we can manage without you.
Forgive us that we play our part
in condemning millions to starvation and death.

Yet help us never to forget that
material well-being is not enough.
Help us to desire above everything else
the self-giving ways of your kingdom,
and to live more simply
so that others may simply live.

Grant that, through the constant expression of
    our gratitude,
we may never take your love for granted.
May we trust in your generous provision –
for today and for ever.
Amen.

Ben Whitney

171 Loving God, you provide all that is good for us.
We thank you for the food and water we are
        about to take.
We pray that those with abundance may
        remember to thank you,
and we especially pray for those who have
        nothing but empty plates and dirty cups.
In Jesus' name we pray.
Amen.

Anna Chang Wright

Formal and institutional graces

Research into eating habits tends to show that families are less likely than in the past to sit down to meals together, which may account for the younger generation's lack of familiarity with saying grace. However, many schools, especially boarding schools, colleges that have formal dinners, and other organizations in which a formal meal is part of their regular activities, often have special graces. Sometimes these are written for each occasion. Sometimes they are ancient graces handed down from the Middle Ages, such as the College Latin graces on pages 47–9. Here is a selection.

172   O Lord, by whom all our wants are supplied,
        and from whom cometh every good and perfect gift;
        we acknowledge with thankful hearts these and
             all thy mercies.
        May we improve them to thy glory;
        through Jesus Christ our Lord.
        Amen.

William Bayley, 1854, for The Clothworkers' Company

173 Give us thankful hearts, O Lord God,
for the table which thou hast spread before us.
Bless thy good creatures to our use,
and us to thy service,
for Jesus Christ his sake.
Amen.

Christ's Hospital School, Horsham, Sussex

174 Lord, relieve the wants of others
and give us grateful hearts;
through Jesus Christ our Lord,
Amen.

Duke of York's Royal Military School, Dover

175 God be praised
for these and all his mercies;
through Jesus Christ our Lord.
Amen.

Duke of York's Royal Military School, Dover

176 In the balance sheet of life we are round this table
nicely in surplus.
We acknowledge this is more by grace than our
own good management.

We bring to mind those many less well resourced
    than ourselves,
for whom neither markets nor central planning
    have filled their supply chain.
For this food, our fellowship, and for the
    managers, workers, business processes
and quality management systems that have
    made possible this occasion,
let us give thanks.
Amen.

Arthur Francis, for a business school dinner

177   To thee, O God, the mighty Lord, most high,
who dost our wants with liberal hand supply,
our grateful hearts and voices now we raise,
to heaven's high throne we chant our hymn of praise,
we bless, we praise, we magnify thy name,
now and henceforth for evermore.
Amen.

J. W. Hobbs, 1855, for The Clothworkers' Company

178   For food and fellowship,
we thank thee, Lord.
Amen.

Traditional, meetings grace

179 Lord, bless all gathered here,
    our fellowship with thee held dear.
    Grant that our meal and meeting may be blest,
    with thee our ever unseen guest.

    Traditional, meetings grace

180 Creator God, bless this food
    through which you recreate our bodies.
    May this time of prayer recreate our souls
    and this food shared help us to recreate our
        world.

    Mount St Mary's Abbey, alt.

181 Receive our thanks for night and day,
    for food and shelter, rest and play.
    Be here our guest and with us stay.
    Amen.

    Refuge blessing

182 God save the Queen and bless our bread.

    Thought to be a Royal Navy grace

183 For friends, good food and wine and fun,
    for the sailing season now begun,

for winds and tides and summer days,
accept, O Lord, our thanks and praise.
Amen.

Elizabeth Lavers, for the Royal Thames Yacht Club
first dinner of the new season, 2008

184 Bless us, O Lord, for these thy gifts, which we are
      about to receive from thy bounty;
through Christ our Lord.
Amen.

Traditional Catholic school grace

185 Almighty God, Lord of heaven and earth,
in whom we live and move and have our being,
we beseech thee to send thine abundant blessing
      upon the earth
that it may bring forth its fruits in due season;
and grant that we, being filled with thy bounty,
may evermore give thanks unto thee, who art the
      giver of all good;
through Jesus Christ our Lord.

The Westcott House Grace, by Brooke Foss Westcott,
1825–1901, Westcott House, Cambridge

Special occasions

Often there is a member of the clergy attending a special occasion who can be relied upon to produce an appropriate grace – but even clergy appreciate a little help. Sometimes it's simply fun to have a special grace to say to make an occasion feel even more special. So here is a selection of occasion-appropriate graces.

186　Father, we thank you for all you provide:
　　　　food for our bodies,
　　　　friends by our side.
　　　　Bless all who this day
　　　　our food have prepared.
　　　　Help us to praise you
　　　　for our daily bread.
　　　　Cindy Gibbons

187　Thank you, Lord, for the blue skies over us,
　　　　the green grass under us,
　　　　and the good friends here with us.

We thank you, God, for the good food in front of us
and ask your blessing on our picnic.
Amen.

Anonymous picnic grace

188 Our Father in heaven,
        we give thanks for the pleasure
        of gathering together for this occasion.
     We give thanks for this food prepared by loving
            hands.
     We give thanks for life,
        the freedom to enjoy it all,
        and all other blessings.
     As we partake of this food,
        we pray for health and strength to carry on
        to try to live as you would have us.
     This we ask in the name of Christ.
     Amen.

Harry Jewell, mid 1900s

Weddings

189 Heavenly Father, we ask you to bless this food
            and those who prepared it and those who
            will serve it.

We also ask your blessing on [*bride's name*] and
 [*bridegroom's name*],
who have come to you this day to unite
  themselves to you in love and sacrament, and
  upon their families.
In Jesus' love.
Amen.

Don Muench

190 Lord Jesus Christ, we thank you for the food
   we share [*tonight*],
in celebration of [*bride's name*] and
 [*bridegroom's name*]'s marriage.
We thank you for the love, guidance and support
  of our parents, family and friends.
We thank you for making this day so enjoyable,
and pray that you will bless those that have
  worked hard to make this day a success for
  [*bride's name*] and [*bridegroom's name*].
Thank you, Lord, for the freedom we have in our
  lives and the beautiful country we enjoy it in.
Heavenly Father, we ask this blessing for the
  newly married couple;
May their love be firm, and may their dream of

life together be a river between two shores –
by day bathed in sunlight, and by night
illuminated from within.
May the heron carry news of them to the heavens,
and the salmon bring the sea's blue grace.
May their twin thoughts spiral upward like
leafy vines, like fiddle strings in the wind,
and be as noble as the Douglas fir.
May they never find themselves back to back
without love pulling them around into
each other's arms.
Amen.

B. J. Murphy; second half James Bertolino, alt.

Christmas

191 O God, our Father,
as we remember the birth of your Son, Jesus Christ,
we welcome him with gladness as Saviour
and pray that there may always be room for him
in our hearts and in our homes;
for his sake.
Amen.

M. H. Botting's collection

192 Let us thank God for Christmas.
For this happy and exciting time of the year,
   thank you, loving Father.
For Christmas trees and decorations,
   thank you, loving Father.
For cards and presents and good food,
   thank you, loving Father.
For fun with family and friends,
   thank you, loving Father.
For singing carols and listening to the
     Christmas story,
   thank you, loving Father.
For all these things
because we have them to remind us of the coming
     of Jesus,
   thank you, loving Father.

John D. Searle

Thanksgiving

193 With heads bowed in gratitude,
with hearts to God upraised –
we gather here together
to offer thanks and praise.

Your blessings fill our table,
your presence warms this place –
as we celebrate Thanksgiving
with these actions of grace.

Yet tomorrow is no different,
for lasting joy abides –
as your Holy Spirit fills us
with unending supplies.

We've received your finest gift,
we who know your Son –
Father, Spirit, Jesus
eternally three in one.

Though great is this mystery,
no man shall comprehend –
yet fully you have known us
and we now call you friend.

For ever we will praise you,
on earth and before the throne –
as we come to your banquet table
when you finally call us home.

This feast we can only imagine,
when every knee shall bow –

oh, glorious, on Thanksgiving
to catch a glimpse right now.
Mary Fairchild

194 We come to give you thanks, O God,
    but how can any words be adequate
       to thank you for absolutely everything?
All that we are and all that we have comes
    from you.
Help us to learn the words of praise and
    thanksgiving every day,
as we strive in gratitude to love you more
    and more.
And help us to learn and do those things that will
    lead us and our neighbors
to that Great Thanksgiving Day when all will
    be fed,
and all will understand each other,
and all will have good schools, good jobs,
    and good health care.
Bless this food and use it
   to energize us for your work of justice.
Amen.
Cathy Stentzel

195   O most merciful Father,
      who hast blessed the labours of the husbandman
      and given unto us the fruits of the earth in their
          season:
      we give thee humble and hearty thanks for this
          thy bounty;
      and we beseech thee to continue this thy
          loving-kindness toward us,
      that year by year, our land may yield her increase,
      to thy glory and our comfort;
      through Jesus Christ our Lord.

American Prayer Book 1792 when there was appointed 'A Day of Thanksgiving to Almighty God, for the Fruits of the Earth, and all other blessings of his merciful Providence'

Harvest

196   We thank you, God, for the harvest of all
          good things;
      for making plants to grow in the earth;
      for giving men strength to work;
      for supplying the food we have each day.
      Teach us to use your gifts fairly and generously

and to remember that you gave them to us;
in the name of Jesus Christ.
Amen.

Christopher Idle

197 As we see the gifts brought here to remind us of
        God's kindness,
    let us give him thanks for the food we eat.
    For food which grows in gardens –
    lettuces, beans, carrots and tomatoes: for these gifts,
        we thank you, God our Father.
    For fields of peas, potatoes, cabbages and
        sugar beet: for these gifts,
        we thank you, God our Father.
    For crops of wheat and the flour for making
        bread and cakes: for these gifts,
        we thank you, God our Father.
    For apples and pears and plums grown in
        orchards: for these gifts,
        we thank you, God our Father.
    For the harvest of the sea – fish and crabs and
        shrimps: for these gifts,
        we thank you, God our Father.

For food from other lands – bananas and oranges
    and fruit in tins: for these gifts,
  we thank you, God our Father.
For the work of farmers, fishermen, shopkeepers
    and all who provide the things we need:
  for these gifts,
  we thank you, God our Father.
We thank you, God our Father, for your love in
    giving so much to us.
Help us to remember that your gifts are meant
    for everyone.
Help us to find ways of sharing with those who
    are poor or hungry.
For your love's sake.
Amen.

John D. Searle

198 We praise the one who gave the growth,
  with voices full and strong.
  Amen.

Walker's Southern Harmony, *1835*

Easter

199   O God, our Father,
     we thank you for this happy day.
     We thank you for Easter eggs and cards
     and for being on holiday.
     We thank you because these things remind us
     of the true meaning of Easter.
     We remember with gladness:
     that Jesus overcame death and showed himself
          to his friends:
          we praise you:
          we thank you.
     That he is alive for evermore:
          we praise you:
          we thank you.
     That he is with us now to be our friend:
          we praise you:
          we thank you.
     That he will always be with us, to the end of time:
          we praise you:
          we thank you.
     Thank you, Lord God, for the good news of Easter.
     Amen.

John D. Searle`

Sung graces

Sung grace is not just the province of the monastic creation of glorious harmonies that might end up on CDs in the Classic Top Ten. Lots of people sing grace including Scouts, Guides, everyone on church camps and ordinary people who just happen to know graces and the tunes that go with them.

200 The Lord is good to me,
     and so I thank the Lord
     for giving me the things I need,
     the sun, the rain, and the appleseed.
     The Lord is good to me.

     And every seed that grows
     will grow into a tree.
     And one day soon
     there'll be apples there
     for everyone in the world to share.
     The Lord is good to me.
     The Johnny Appleseed grace

201 All good gifts around us
      are sent from heaven above;
      then thank the Lord,
      Oh thank the Lord,
      for all his love.
      Amen.

Matthias Claudius, 1740–1815

202 Thank you, Lord, for this food.
      We remember the giver.
      May we all, each one and all,
      Praise his great name for ever.

Sung to the tune of 'Edelweiss'

203 Praise God from whom all blessings flow,
      praise him all creatures here below,
      praise him above, ye heavenly host,
      praise Father, Son and Holy Ghost.

Thomas Ken, 1637–1711

204 For the beauty of the earth,
  for the glory of the skies,
  for the love which from our birth
  over and around us lies,
  God of all, to you we raise
  this our prayer of grateful praise.

  For the beauty of each hour,
  of the day and of the night,
  hill and vale, and tree and flower,
  sun and moon, and stars of light,
  God of all, to you we raise
  this our prayer of grateful praise.

  For the joy of human love,
  brother, sister, parent, child,
  friends on earth and friends above,
  for all gentle thoughts and mild,
  God of all, to you we raise
  this our prayer of grateful praise.
  Amen.

  Folliott Sandford Pierpoint, 1835–1917, alt.

205 God is good, God is great
  and we thank him for our food.

We're going to thank him morning, noon and night.
We thank you, Lord, because you're out of sight.
Amen, amen, amen, amen, amen.

Sung to the tune of 'Rock around the Clock' (Australian Scouts' grace)

206 Thank you, Lord, for giving us food!
    [*Raise left arm in a punch as if flying like Superman*]
    Thank you, Lord, for giving us food!
    [*As above with right arm*]
    Our daily bread, we must be fed!
    [*Sway arms around as if steering through the air*]
    Thank you, Lord, for giving us food!
    [*Actions as first line*]
    Thank you, Lord, for giving as food!
    [*As second line*]

    Sung with actions to Superman *theme tune by Australian church camps*

207 To God who gives our daily bread
    a thankful song we raise,
    and pray that he who sends us food
    may fill our hearts with praise.

    Thomas Tallis, c. 1505–85

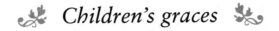 Children's graces

I've been interested to discover that there are quite large numbers of contemporary graces for children compared with those for adults. I suppose one of the earliest things one tries to teach children is to say 'Please' and 'Thank you', so it's quite logical that they should be taught to say thank you to God. However, I wonder whether this is a case of 'Do as I say, not as I do'.

208 Father high in heaven
     all by thee are fed;
     hear thy children praise thee
     for our daily bread.

Anonymous

209 Rub a dub dub [*circling motion on tummy*],
     thanks for the grub.

Anonymous

210 Before I take my pleasant food
     I'll thank thee, Lord, who is so good
     in sending all I need: now, Lord,
     be pleased, I entreat,
     to bless the food
     that I may eat
     and be my constant friend.
     A Child's Verse-Book of Devotions, *1840*

211 O Lord, I thank thee, who dost give
     the daily bread by which I live;
     Oh, bless the food I now partake
     and save my soul for Jesus' sake.
     A Child's Verse-Book of Devotions, *1840*

212 Thank you for all the good food you give us,
     and for all the shop people
     who keep it ready for us in their shops.
     Christopher D. Bacon

Breakfast graces

213   Thank you, Father God,
for our breakfast today.
Thank you for cornflakes
and an egg
and milk to drink
and bread and butter.*
Thank you for our mummies [or big brothers
     or sisters]*
who got breakfast for us.

Christopher D. Bacon

*Adapt as necessary

214   Dear Father God,
we like to have a nice egg for breakfast
and some toast to dip in it.
Thank you for the hens which lay the eggs,
and the farmers who feed the hens,
and the shops where we see lots of eggs in boxes.
Thank you for all nice things to eat.

Christopher D. Bacon

Thank you for everything!

215 For our warm homes,
   the food we eat,
   the clothes we wear,
   our cosy beds,
   thank you, God.

   Christopher D. Bacon

216 Dear Father,
   you have given us good food and clean houses;
   you have often kept us safe from accidents
   and cured us when we were ill.
   We are sorry we have never thanked you enough
   for all you have done for us.
   Amen.

   from Family Prayers, *1971*

217 God, we thank you for this food,
   for rest and home and all things good,
   for wind and rain and sun above,
   but most of all for those we love.

   Maryleona Frost

218 We thank thee, Lord, for happy hearts,
for rain and sunny weather.
We thank thee, Lord, for this our food,
and that we are together.

Emilie Fendall Johnson

219 Thank you for the world so sweet,
thank you for the food we eat,
thank you for the birds that sing,
thank you, Lord, for everything.

Edith Rutter Leatham, 1870–1939

Birthdays

220 Jesus, we know you had birthdays just like us.
We don't know if you had special food or parties
but we know you liked nice food
and you used to go to parties,
so we invite you to be at this party
and bless us as we are sharing the fun
and the food
and the presents.
Amen.

Dorothy M. Stewart

221 Thank you, Father God,
        for birthdays.
     Thank you for presents
     and special treats
     and parties
     to make our birthdays happy.
     Christopher D. Bacon

Christmas

222 Happy birthday, Jesus.
     Thank you that we can share in celebrating your
         special day.
     Be with us and bless us.
     Amen.
     Dorothy M. Stewart

223 Thank you, Father God, for Christmas –
     for Christmas trees
     and Christmas cards
     and Christmas presents
     and Christmas dinner
     and all our happy times.
     Christopher D. Bacon

Graces from other faiths and none

It would be offensive to suggest that Christianity is the only faith that recognizes a need to give thanks for food and other blessings. There is a rich seam of thanksgiving in other faiths, philosophies and even in people of no faith at all. Here is a selection of such thanks.

224 Lord most giving and resourceful, I implore you:
     make it your will that this people enjoy
     the goods and riches you naturally give,
     that naturally issue from you,
     that are pleasing and savoury,
     that delight and comfort,
     though lasting but briefly,
     passing away as if in a dream.

Aztec, c. 1500s

225 This plate of food,
     so fragrant and appetizing,
     also contains much suffering.

Buddhist

226 We return thanks to our Mother, the earth,
which sustains us.
We return thanks to the rivers and streams,
which supply us with water.
We return thanks to all herbs,
which furnish medicines for the cure of our
diseases.
We return thanks to the corn, and to her sisters,
the beans and squashes,
which give us life.
We return thanks to the wind,
which, moving the air, has banished diseases.
We return thanks to the moon and stars,
which have given to us their light when the sun
was gone.
We return thanks to the sun,
which has looked upon the earth with a
beneficent eye.
Lastly, we return thanks to the Great Spirit,
in whom is embodied all goodness,
and who directs all things for the good of his
children.
Amen.

Iroquois

227 Truly now,
    double thanks, triple thanks,
    that we've been formed,
    we've been given mouths, our faces,
    we speak, we listen, we wonder, we move.
    Our knowledge is good,
    we've understood what it is for.
    We hear and we've seen
    what is great and small
    under the sky and on the earth.

Mayan

228 Praise be to him,
    who when I call on him answers me,
    slow though I am when he calls me.
    Praise be to him,
    who gives to me when I ask him,
    miserly though I am when he asks something
        of me.
    Praise be to him to whom I confide my needs
    and he satisfies them.
    My Lord, I praise thee,
    for thou art of my praise most worthy.

Muslim

229 For carpaccio, chicken and blueberry pud,
       give praise and thanksgiving to whomever
              you would.
       Amen.

Arthur Francis

230 *Yā devī sarvabhūtesu ksudhārūpena samsthitā
        namastasyai namastasyai namastasyai namo
        namah.*

       I bow down to that Goddess who lives within
              every body in the form of hunger.

Sanskrit, 11th/12th century

231 Grandfather Great Spirit,
       all that we have and are
       has come up out of the ground.
       Fill us with the light.
       Give us the strength to understand,
       the eyes to see,
       the hearts to receive,
       and teach us to walk the soft earth
       as relative to all that live.
       Amen.

Sioux, alt.

232 From too much love of living,
from hope and fear set free,
we thank with brief thanksgiving
whatever gods may be.

Algernon Charles Swinburne, 1837–1909

233 Salutations! O merciful God,
who provides food for the body and soul,
you have kindly granted what is spread before us.
We thank you.
Bless the loving hands that prepared this meal
and us, who are to enjoy it.
Homage, homage, homage to thee!

Tamil, Manikka Vasahar, 8th century

234 We give thanks
for all green and growing things:
for the nuts and the fruit,
for the leaf and the root,
for the hops on the vine,
for the bread and the wine.

Vegetarian grace, Sandy Spirling

235 We give thanks for this food:
     grown from the bounty of the earth,
     blessed by the warmth of the sun,
     given nourishment by the rain,
     pollinated by the wind
     and prepared lovingly by these hands.
     May we use it well.

     Kaaren Whitney

236 For these and all thy blessings
     so kindly bestowed upon us,
     our most sincere thanks,
     dear Ahura Mazda.

     Zoroaster, 700–600 BC

 *Grace after food*

When it comes to food, I wonder what difference it makes when we say our thank yous to God – before or after a meal. Some traditions do both. Here are a couple of post-prandial prayers.

237 Dear Lord,
     I'm a little late,
     but do please bless the food I ate.
     Anonymous

238 Thank you, Lord, for what we've had.
     If there'd been more, I would have been glad.
     Anonymous

Acknowledgements

The compiler and publishers are pleased to acknowledge the authors and publishers of the works listed below for permission to quote from their copyrighted material. Special thanks are due to those authors whose work is being published here for the first time. Numbers refer to the prayer numbers.

10 In A. S. T. Fisher, *An Anthology of Prayers* (Longmans, Green & Co., 1934).

15, 25, 150, 216 © Scripture Union, from *Family Prayers* 1971 by Mary Batchelor, Derek J. Prime, Yvonne Simms, Linda C. Taylor and Margaret Wade.

23, 62, 162, 191, 196, 197, 199 From *Prayers for Today's Church*, ed. Dick Williams (Falcon Books/CPAS, 1972), with permission, <www.cpas.org.uk>.

31 Allan Denholm.

32 Gipsy prayer, Week 39, 24 September, *All the Glorious Names*, URC Prayer Handbook 1989, ed. Edmund Banyard, published by the United Reformed Church. Used by permission.

34 Veronica Heley.

40 Excerpt from 'Give us this bread!' by Michael and Susan Durber, 17 November, *For the Love of God*, URC Prayer Handbook 1996,

ed. Janet Wootton, published by the United Reformed Church. Used by permission.

41 Andrew Mayo.

42 Stephen Orchard, Week 39, 24 September, *All the Glorious Names*, URC Prayer Handbook 1989, ed. Edmund Banyard, published by the United Reformed Church. Used by permission.

43 David Jenkins, top of third page of Personal Prayers section at end of *The Word and the World,* URC Prayer Handbook 1986, ed. Edmund Banyard, published by the United Reformed Church. Used by permission.

44 Chris Warner, last paragraph p. 58, 12 April, from *Shining Faces,* URC Prayer Handbook 2000–2001, ed. Janet Lees, published by the United Reformed Church. Used by permission.

45, 46 Jean Mortimor, last 2 lines, second page of Week 15, 14 April, and excerpt (2nd last paragraph) from 'Food for Thought' in *Exceeding Our Limits,* URC Prayer Handbook 1991, ed. Graham J. Cook, published by the United Reformed Church. Used by permission.

47 Clare McBeath, excerpt from 'Food of Angels', last 6 lines, p. 104, 6 August, in *Justice, Joy and Jubilee,* URC Prayer Handbook 1999–2000, ed. Janet Lees, published by the United Reformed Church. Used by permission.

48 Michael and Susan Durber, excerpt from 'Water into wine', 21 January, in *For the Love of God*, URC Prayer Handbook 1996, ed. Janet Wootton, published by the United Reformed Church. Used by permission.

49 Excerpt from 'The food of love', 28 July, in *For the Love of God* (see 48).

52 Excerpt from 'Praise the Lord' (first 8 lines) by Chris Campbell, 30 January, p. 32, *Justice, Joy and Jubilee*, URC Prayer Handbook 1999–2000, ed. Janet Lees, published by the United Reformed Church. Used by permission.

53 Melanie Frew, excerpt (last 3 lines) from 'We have heard . . .', p. 134, 19 November, *Justice, Joy and Jubilee*, URC Prayer Handbook 1999–2000, ed. Janet Lees, published by the United Reformed Church. Used by permission.

56 Stephen Orchard, Week 3, 15 January, in *All the Glorious Names*, URC Prayer Handbook 1989, ed. Edmund Banyard, published by the United Reformed Church. Used by permission.

58 BRF (<www.brf.org.uk>) for the extract from *Quiet Spaces: The Feast*, 2005, 'Bible meals' p. 14, the article being an edited extract from *Feasting on God's Word* (BRF, 2002) by David Spriggs.

66 Brian Wren, from *Christian Aid Prayers 1980* in *Bread of Tomorrow*, ed. Janet Morley (SPCK/Christian Aid, 1992), pp. 161–2, no. 20, first verse.

90, 91 Kirsten Weissenberg for the English translations of traditional German prayers from Olaf Schmidt's website <www.amen-online.de/gebet/tageszeiten/tischgebete/traditionell.htm>.

100 Ethiopian Orthodox prayer, alt., 7 February, p. 35, from *Gateways of Grace*, URC Prayer Handbook 1998–9, ed. Janet Lees, published by the United Reformed Church. Used by permission.

101 Keith and Margaret Rowbory.

102, 103, 104 Joy Cowley, *Psalms Down Under*, 1996, Pleroma, New Zealand.

121, 123 Extracts from the Authorized Version of the Bible (The

King James Bible), the rights in which are vested in the Crown, are reproduced by permission of the Crown's Patentee, Cambridge University Press.

124, 126, 129, 130 Simon Baynes for permission to reproduce the appendix of graces based on Bible verses from his book, *A Bible Prayer Book*.

161 © Jan Berry in *Bread of Tomorrow*, ed. Janet Morley (SPCK/Christian Aid, 1992), pp. 173–4.

164 © Tony Burnham, 'Feeding the five billion', right-hand page, Week 4, 28 January, *Say one for me!*, URC Prayer Handbook 1990, eds Tony Burnham and Graham Cook, published by the United Reformed Church. Used by permission.

165 'Meal Blessing' by Christina J. DelPiero, pp. 37–8, in *Women Pray*, Karen L. Roller (The Pilgrim Press, 1986) by kind permission of The Pilgrim Press.

166 Janet Morley, from *All Desires Known* (SPCK, 1992) in *Bread of Tomorrow*, ed. Janet Morley (SPCK/Christian Aid, 1992) p. 184, no. 16.

167 Larry Pugh for permission to use this thanksgiving prayer by his father, Samuel F. Pugh.

169 Tasha Tudor, *First Graces* (Lutterworth Press, 1964, 1991), p. 40, by kind permission of Lutterworth Press.

170 Ben Whitney, *Through Darkened Glass* (Epworth Press, 1987), 'Food', p. 55.

171 Anna Chang Wright.

174, 175 Charles Johnson, Headmaster, Duke of York's Royal Military School, Dover.

176 Professor Arthur Francis, Dean, Bradford University School of Management.

183 Elizabeth Lavers.

186 Cynthia Boreham, who writes as Cindy Gibbons.

189 Donald Muench.

190 John Murphy; James Bertolino.

193 Mary Fairchild (for more articles and poetry by Mary Fairchild, visit <www.christianity.about.com>).

194 The Revd Cathy Stentzel.

212, 213, 214, 215, 221, 223 Christian Education for prayers from *Praying with Beginners* by Christopher and Margaret Bacon (Chester House Publications by arrangement with the National Christian Education Council, 1968).

218 Ms Maud Petersham for prayer by Emilie Fendall Johnson, from *A Little Book of Prayers* (The Viking Press, NY, 1941).

229 Professor Arthur Francis, Dean, Bradford University School of Management.

234 Sandy Spirling.

235 Kaaren Whitney.

A special word of thanks to those who supplied graces, encouragement, explanations and sources: first to my husband, John Courtis, who emailed around 180 friends and contacts requesting contributions for the book, and also to Barbara Arnold; Larry Adams; Angela at Floris Books; Professor Sir John Baker; Mike Bannister; John Barnes; Susan Baxendale of Methodist Publishing

House; Kathryn Bones; Katy Bull; St Catharine's College, Cambridge; Tim Chambers of <www.purl.org/net/tbc/mealpryr.htm>; Anne Charleston; Robert Clinton; Len Collinson; Ian Courtis; Jane Courtis; Paula Craik at the Institute of Chartered Accountants of Scotland; Bishop Andrew W. Curnow of Bendigo Diocese, Australia; Siobhan Daiko; Roy Davidson; Oliver de la Paz; Luke Deal and Nigel Lungley of BBC Radio Suffolk; Michael Denton; Patsy Dittes; Lisa Dowdeswell at the Society of Authors; Audrey Drake; Keith Fowler of Woodbridge; Jonny Gallant at St Andrew's Press; James and Morna Gemmell; the Revd Christine Haddon-Reece and David Haddon-Reece; Ailsa Hamilton; Yvonne Haramis; Keith Harrison; Charles P. Henderson of <www.god-web.org>; Eric Hodges; David W. Holt; Adele Hudson; Pauline Hyde; Nicholas C. Jenkins; Michael Julien; Philip Law; Marjorie Lewis; Ron Little; Celeste Lotz; Vincent Lugthart; Jill and Alistair Macfarlane; Mrs Maclean of the Steiner School, Edinburgh; Ailsa Marks; Pat Moxey; Fiona Murphy at Transworld Publishers; Alison Nichols; Linda Norris; James Oates; Pat Rae; Niels Rakhorst; Rob at ALCS; Barbara Robertson; Elona Rogers; Julian Rogers; Roberta Rominger; Ann Rowbory; Keith and Margaret Rowbory; David Say; Claire Scott; the Revd Greg Smith, Chair, Huron Hunger Fund; Maggie Smith; Raymond M. Smith; Naomi Starkey; Valerie Stewart; John Stork; Anne Taute; Richard Taylor of the Recruitment Society; Richard Thornburgh; Nick Wain; Kaaren Whitney; James Knox Whittet; Pat Wood.

Index of authors

Note: The numbers shown are the prayer numbers.

Agnes, St 8
Albert, Prince-Consort 131
American Prayer Book 195
Anonymous 1, 5, 7, 10, 12, 14, 27, 28, 30, 50, 160, 187, 208, 209, 237, 238
Appleseed, Johnny 200
Augustine, St 132
Austin, Alfred 51

Bacon, Christopher D. 212, 213, 214, 215, 221, 223
Bayley, William 172
Baynes, Simon 124, 126, 129, 130
Bellin, George 20, 149
Berry, Jan 161

Bertolino, James 190
Botting, M. H. 162, 191
Brigid (Bride) 86
Burnham, Tony 164
Burns, Robert 74, 75

Campbell, Chris 52
Cennick, John 159
Chrysostom, St John 143
Clarke, Jeremiah 154
Claudius, Matthias 201
Clement of Alexandria 141
Cowley, Joy 102, 103, 104

DelPiero, Christina J. 165
Denholm, Allan 31
Donne, John 11
Durber, Michael and Susan 40, 48, 49

Eckhart, Meister 133
Eisenhower, President Dwight D. 134
Emerson, Ralph Waldo 108
Ephraem the Syrian 142
Erasmus, Desiderius 135

Fairchild, Mary 193
Francis, Arthur 176, 229
Francis of Assisi, St 136
Frew, Melanie 53
Frost, Maryleona 217

Gibbons, Cindy 186
grandfather, Veronica Heley's 34
Guest, Edgar A. 33

Heard, Josephine Delphine Henderson 109

Heley, Veronica 34
Henry, Matthew 9
Herbert, George 155
Herrick, Robert 151, 152
Hobbs, J. W. 177
Hodge 35

Idle, Christopher 196

Jenkins, David 43
Jewell, Harry 188
Johnson, Emilie Fendall 218

Ken, Thomas 203

Lavers, Elizabeth 183
Leatham, Edith Rutter 219
Lotz, Celeste 26
Luther, Martin 92, 119

McBeath, Claire 47
Marot, Clément 89
Mayo, Andrew 41
Monsell, John Samuel Bewley 54
More, Thomas 137
Morley, Janet 166
Mortimor, Jean 45, 46
Moody, Dwight L. 21
Muench, Don 189
Murphy, B. J. 190

Newton, John 158
Norden, J. 55

Orchard, Stephen 42, 56

Patmore, Coventry 22
Petrov, Gregory 95
Pierpoint, Folliott Sandford 204
Procter, Adelaide Anne 57
Pugh, Samuel F. 167

Rowbory, Keith and Margaret 101

St Agnes 8
St Augustine 132
St Francis of Assisi 136
St John Chrysostom 143
Scottish minister 37
Searle, John D. 192, 197, 199
Shakespeare, William 138
Sorsky, Nilus 96
Spirling, Sandy 234
Spriggs, David 58
Stentzel, Cathy 194
Stevenson, Robert Louis 139

Stewart, Dorothy M. 220, 222
Strong, Nathaniel 156
Street, F. W. 23
Swinburne, Algernon Charles 232

Tallis, Thomas 207
Taylor, Jane 59
Tudor, Tasha 169
Turner, H. W. 61

Walton, Izaak 153
Warner, Andrew 62
Warner, Chris 44
Watts, Isaac 18
Webb, Thomas H. B. 64
Weissenberg, Kirsten 90, 91
Wesley, Charles 140
Westcott, Brooke Foss 185
Whitney, Ben 170
Whitney, Kaaren 235
Wilson, Thomas 157
Wordsworth, Christopher 65
Wren, Brian 66
Wright, Anna Chang 171

Zoroaster 236

Index of first lines

Note: The numbers shown are the prayer numbers.

All good gifts around us 201
All praise and glory is due to thee, O God 156
All you big things, bless the Lord 99
Alle guten Gaben 90
Almighty God, eternal King 149
Almighty God, Lord of heaven and earth 185
As food is shared among us 49
As to the different kinds of food 96
As we look forward to the glory of your kingdom 53
As we see the gifts brought here to remind us of God's kindness 197
Awadifo, Yesu 101

Be present at our table, Lord 159
Before I take my pleasant food 210
Benedic nobis, Dominum 115
Benedicat nobis 116
Benedicatur 118

Benedictus benedicat 117
Bless me, O Lord 18
Bless the sheep for David's sake 81
Bless these thy gifts, most gracious God 150
Bless this food and us that eats it 6
Bless this food we are about to receive 112
Bless to me, O God 77
Bless us, O God the Father, who hast created us 93
Bless us, O Lord, for these thy gifts 184
Bless, O my soul, the Lord thy God 125
Blessed are you, great God 40
Blessed are you, O Lord our God, eternal King 68
Blessed art thou, O Lord our God, King of the universe 69
Blessed be the Lord 123
Blessed be the Lord God of the universe 70
Blessed be thou, Lord God of the universe 71

Blessed God, who feedest me 143
Blessing to God, for ever blest 140
Blessings on our meal 3
Blessings we enjoy daily, and for the most of them 153
Bountiful God, bless this food 45
Brown bread and the gospel is good fare 9

Come, Lord Jesus, be our guest 13
Come, Lord Jesus, our guest to be 111
Creator God, bless this food 180
Creator God, you have provided us 162

Dear Father God, we like to have a nice egg for breakfast 214
Dear Father, you have given us 216
Dear Lord, bless these sinners 14
Dear Lord, I'm a little late 237
Dear Lord, please don't make us like porridge 29
Dear Lord, thank you for all you have given us 25
Dear Lord, we ask you to bless 26
Dominus Jesus 119
Doon on your hunkers 37

Each time we eat 98
Even though we walk through the darkest valley 122
Every thing I have received, from thee it came 76

Father high in heaven 208
Father, we thank thee for this food 160
Father, we thank you for all you provide 186
For all the glory of the way 63
For all your goodness, God 113
For bread and jam 28
For carpaccio, chicken and blueberry pud 229
For each new morning with its light 108
For every cup and plateful 10
For food and fellowship 178
For food that stays our hunger 60
For friends, family and the roast 12
For friends, good food and wine and fun 183
For health and strength and daily food 16
For life and love, for rest and food 54
For our warm homes 215
For the beauty of the earth 204
For the food we are about to eat 72
For these and all thy blessings 236
For these and all thy mercies given 146
For these and his other mercies 51
For these gifts of food 23
For what we are about to receive 17

Forgive us our hurried,
  inhospitable lifestyle 46
From too much love of living 232

Generous God, thank you for
  feeding us 164
Give me a good digestion, Lord 64
Give thanks to God with one
  accord 19
Give us grace, O God 136
Give us thankful hearts, O Lord
  God 173
God be praised 175
God bless our going out 131
God bless our meat 20
God! If all you are is a swig 32
God is good 27
God is good, God is great 205
God is great 114
God of the earth 165
God our creator, you have made us
  one with this earth 166
God save the Queen and bless our
  bread 182
God send this crumb well down 36
God sends no one away empty 21
God, we thank you for this food
  217
God, you heap your love upon us
  161
God, you nourish and sustain us
  56
God's grace is the only grace 22

Good food 7
Good Lord, for thy grace meekly
  we call 145   – 10. Jan.'
Gracious and glorious 38
Grandfather Great Spirit 231
Great God, accept our gratitude
  109
Great God, thou giver of all good
  154
Great, Pa 2

Happy birthday, Jesus 222
Heavenly Father, bless us 35
Heavenly Father, we ask you to
  bless this food 189
Here a little child I stand 151

I am blessed 67
I ask for the angels of heaven to be
  among us 86
In a world where there is so much
  hunger 163
In the balance sheet of life 176
In the name of the Father 30
It is meet before we partake of
  food 141

Jesus, thank you for loving us 50
Jesus, we know you had birthdays
  just like us 220

*Komm, Herr Jesus, sei du unser
  Gast* 91

Let us thank God for Christmas 192

Life is for living 103

Living Love 66

Lord, behold our family here assembled 139

Lord, bless all gathered here 179

Lord God, people need food 58

Lord, I would own thy tender care 59

Lord Jesus Christ, because you broke bread with the poor 168

Lord Jesus Christ, we thank you for the food we share 190

Lord Jesus Christ, who came to earth that we might have life 62

Lord Jesus, be our holy guest 134

Lord Jesus, be with us in this 92

Lord, make us mindful 126

Lord, make us truly thankful 24

Lord, may we share this meal with the same 43

Lord most giving and resourceful, I implore you 224

Lord, relieve the wants of others 174

Lord, we work mighty hard for these here vittals 107

Loving God, you provide all that is good for us 171

Many grains, many grapes 47

May all we say and all we think 106

May God be praised 11

May God give us grateful hearts 169

May he that feeds all things with his bounty 135

May the blessing 83

May the grace of Christ our Saviour 158

May thy Holy Spirit continually descend 61

My eyes praise the Lord! 52

My God, I thank thee who hast made 57

Now therefore, our God, we thank thee 121

O God, how lovely it is to be your guest 95

O God, our Father, as we remember the birth 191

O God, our Father, we thank you for this happy day 199

O God, when I have food 167

O God, who givest food unto all flesh 157

O God, who makes a thousand flowers to blow 88

O Lord of heaven and earth and sea 65

O Lord, by whom all our wants are supplied 172

O Lord, heap blessings on the soup 31

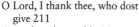

O Lord, I thank thee, who dost give 211
O Lord, make us able 85
O Lord, now bless and bind us 105
O Lord, that lends me life 138
O Lord, thou art my God and King 127
O most merciful Father, who hast blessed 195
O thou light of my heart 132
O thou who kindly dost provide 75
O thou, great giver of all things 104
Oculi omnium in te sperant Domine 120
One word as good as ten 8
Our Father in heaven 188
Our God, for all the good things you provide for us 41
Our God, we are your guests 80

Père eternel, qui nous ordonnes 89
Praise be to him 228
Praise God from whom all blessings flow 203
Praise the Lord and pass the mustard 5
Praise to God who givest meat 39
Pray we to God, the almighty Lord 147
Provider God 170

Receive our thanks for night and day 181

Rub a dub dub 209

Salutations! O merciful God 233
Satisfied, O Lord, with the gifts of thy riches 144
Some hae meat and canna eat 74

Thank Heaven for this food 94
Thank you for all the good food you give us 212
Thank you for the miracle of a good wine 48
Thank you for the wind and rain 110
Thank you for the world so sweet 219
Thank you, Father God, for birthdays 221
Thank you, Father God, for Christmas 223
Thank you, Father God, for our breakfast today 213
Thank you, God, for blue skies above 82
Thank you, Lord 1
Thank you, Lord, for giving us food! 206
Thank you, Lord, for our daily bread 129
Thank you, Lord, for rain and fruitful seasons 130
Thank you, Lord, for the blue skies over us 187
Thank you, Lord, for this food 202

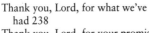
Thank you, Lord, for what we've had 238

Thank you, Lord, for your promise of old 124

The eyes of all things do look up and trust in thee, O Lord 148

The eyes of all wait upon thee 128

The food we have here is a gift 102

The Lord be praised! 34

The Lord is good to me 200

The Sacred Three be blessing thee 84

The Sacred Three my fortress be 78

There is no such thing as 'my' bread 133

These things, good Lord, that we pray for 137

This plate of food 225

Thou who hast given so much to me 155

Though our mouths were full of song as the sea 73

To God who gives our daily bread 207

To thee, O God, the mighty Lord, most high 177

Truly now 227

Us 4

We ask thy blessing, gracious God, as we sit together 87

We come to give you thanks, O God 194

We give thanks for all green and growing things 234

We give thanks for this food 235

We praise the one who gave the growth 198

We pray that as we share this meal 44

We return thanks to our Mother, the earth 226

We thank thee, Lord, for happy hearts 218

We thank you for our food 42

We thank you, God, for the harvest of all good things 196

What God gives, and what we take 152

Whatever we do, you are with us 55

When turkey's on the table laid 33

With bread and wine 97

With heads bowed in gratitude 193

Without your sunshine and your rain 79

Yā devī sarvabhūtesu 230

You are the guest who filled the jars with good wine 142

You have created all creatures with your word 100

You have given us so much, Lord 15